Contents

C000077369

Kin

Karl Knights

NEW**POETS**LIST

the poetry business

Published 2022 by
New Poets List
An imprint of The Poetry Business
Campo House,
54 Campo Lane,
Sheffield S1 2EG

ISBN 978-1-914914-28-7
eBook ISBN 978-1-914914-29-4
Typeset by The Poetry Business
Printed by Biddles, Sheffield

Smith|Doorstop Books are a member of Inpress:
www.inpressbooks.co.uk

Distributed by IPS UK, 1 Deltic Avenue,
Rooksley, Milton Keynes MK13 8LD

The Poetry Business gratefully acknowledges the support
of Arts Council England.

Supported using public funding by
ARTS COUNCIL
ENGLAND
LOTTERY FUNDED

For all my kin

Growing Pains

I didn't know I was disabled.
I thought everyone went home
and sat in their wheelchairs.

*

The extra pair
of boxers and trousers
in the back of my school bag.

*

A fight in the playground,
he kicks my leg,
hits the splint. I smile.

*

The black woman in the mobility scooter
ruffled my spiky hair. She was the first
to see me, not the chair.

*

The old man in the electric wheelchair
joking outside the hospital toilets
'Don't go taking this for a ride.'

*

My parents give me a bear
with a lab coat and thermometer
from the hospital gift shop.

*

The first kiss and she says
'I'm surprised
you can kiss.'

*

'Why do you like the hospital?'
'Nobody stares at me here.'

I Have a Literal Mind

Dad tells me to pull my socks up
and I yank them till they rip.

A teacher says take a seat,
I pick up the chair and walk out.

A Speech Impediment

Like his tongue was a snake
he told me. That year, I was his translator
and occasional censor. The Head said
'*What* did he call me?'

We never spoke of it.
He didn't ask about my legs
and I didn't ask about his mouth,
that was the gift.

The Difference Between a Dog and a Biscuit Tin

It's Boxing Day and I'm nearly ten and a half.
I got the camouflaged Action Man for Christmas.
I told Mum I wanted to open it on my own,
but my special scissors won't cut the plastic.
Just as I start to stick my tongue out and sweat,
Mum calls my name from the front room.
I shuffle down the stairs on my bum.
Mum says I should use the stairlift.
She taps me on the shoulder and says
'Look at the telly! This film's got a boy like you.
See? He even flaps his hands like you. He's called Kyle.'
On the screen a man and a woman stand
in a kitchen that looks bigger than ours.
Her scarf is the same colour as my blue badge.
The man rubs his face with his big hands and says
Whatever happened Nic, whatever happened to us?
Kyle happened. Mum tells me to pay attention
but the screen's too bright. The man is now standing
in front of a house that posh people have.
He shouts too loudly, *For God's sake it's autism,*
he doesn't know what love is.
He can't tell the difference
between a dog and a biscuit tin.
Mum pulls my hands from my ears
and points toward the person she thinks I am.

How to Wheel

The zoo is tough terrain; hilly.
I wheel as fast as I can –
then Mum shouts 'Keep up!'
I stop. 'Hand me my crutches.'
I shakily get up; tear off my splints'
velcro straps, and put them on her.
I sit her in the chair. 'You have a go.'

At first, she spins in circles.
'No,' I say. 'Use both arms in unison.'
She still veers away, zigzagging, sweating now.
People start to stare. She blushes,
keeps her head down. After ten minutes
she's heaving, shirt drenched.
I swing over to her.

Pushing My Sister

Jake doesn't know how to push
so it's me again, holding
your wheelchair handles
and pushing to the shop.
He doesn't know that you must
mount a kerb back wheels first.
He doesn't know how much oomph
you need in the right hand when
the pavements slant. Like Dad,
he doesn't listen when we say
'Never tip me up, and *no* wheelies.'
When the gawks start to come
and my hands tighten, you tell me
about the group of girls who laughed
at you and wouldn't budge
in Ipswich High Street. You shunted
your footrests straight into their shins.
Three years on a waiting list
for an electric wheelchair.
When it's charged, we head out
the door, my hands still
reaching for your handles.

My Wards

The child with a hole in her cheek the size of an exhaust pipe, who rocks
    on the wooden horse.
The father talking about the drive over to his son, reading his first book
    in braille.
The kid learning to walk with his amputated toe, leaning on the nurse's arm.
The quiet outpatient wobbling on her just-fitted prosthetic. She tells her
    mum the liner itches.
The tired nurse who hands a melting Mars bar to the lad coming out of a fit.
The ten-year-old with the wires and pads still attached, recovering from a
    heart attack.
The friend with a horseshoe scar on his skull, chuckling as he runs through
    automatic doors.
The limbless teen on her skateboard, using her stumps to push, crashing
    into the doctor's ankles.
The oldest of us all, practising her breathing exercises, after the flu attacked
    her lungs.
The scream we hear through the wall, the bone marrow donor who can't
    have anaesthetic.

The daughter with smiley face wheel covers, who I meet eye-to-eye buying
    sweets in the gift shop.
The blind man in a suit, passing through, who breaks the rules and lets us
    pet his dog.
The old lady listening to his funeral plans. 'No black, no black at all,' insists
    her grandson.
The mother pressing a tissue to her son's lips, drooping from the stroke.
The loner fed through a tube, glaring at the chatterbox scoffing soggy
    buttered toast in the next bed.
The toddler whose eyeball spilled out onto his cheek, burning it. He rubs
    below the new eye-patch.

The laugh from the lipless joker, his gums always on show. 'Watch me eat a lolly,' he says.

The girl connected to oxygen tanks, trying to finish her bucket list. All she's got is 'kiss a boy.'

The teenager who knows he's dying and doesn't look his dad in the eye.

The voice I never see but always hear – she never stopped singing.

First Meeting

I'd never met another autistic person.
My SENCO wanted me to tutor him.
I was fifteen, he was twelve. I waited for him
in the room we'd been assigned. I could hear
the other SEN kids, laughing and screaming, arguing
with their TAs. Then he came in, Tom. He sat down.
My stims – tapping my teeth,
twiddling my fingers, spinning my keys –
were exactly mirrored. He stared at the floor
as I used to. He fidgeted, bounced,
rocked. He told me he didn't understand
why the girl next to him in Maths
keeps passing notes and smiling?
Why do teachers insist on eye contact
when it means nothing?
I said I didn't know either.
Try and look at their noses, or their foreheads.
I pulled out some of the board games left in our room,
not Monopoly – we sussed we couldn't do numbers.
When the bell rang neither of us knew how to leave.

Physio

'Stand on one leg,' she says.
She rests her hands in the air
around my hips. 'I've got you,
I won't let you fall.'

*

'Walk across the room
and back for me?'
I concentrate, heel
to the ground first,
not toe. 'And again.'

*

Holding my hips,
placing her thumb in the joint
she says 'tuck your bum in.'
The muscle moves around her hand.

*

'The hips are slightly out of place'
she says to my parents.
I look at my sister.
We roll our eyes.

*

Lying on the hard blue mat
I count the ceiling tiles.
'Try to relax,' she'd say
as she gripped my calf,
stretched in her palm.

*

'She'll be shadowing me today,
she's learning. Is that okay?'
When I'm being pulled she turns
to the student and says 'note
the flexion in the right leg. The spasticity.'

*

She places her knee
in the small of my back,
tugs my arms towards her.
'Does that hurt?' Yes.

*

'Stand on your toes for me.
That's much better than we expected.'
And the blue mat, now too small.

The Spastic's Guide to Sex

After Jillian Weise

Step One: Preparation
Before he arrives shove the wheelchair
and night callipers in the cupboard.
Roll your jeans up, take off
your splints, strap by strap,
and lay them under the bed.

Step Two: Foreplay
When he runs his hands over your body
and steps back, shocked how your muscles
are right there on the surface, taut as guitar strings,
don't take it personally. It must be the first time
he's felt a leg like yours.

Step Three: Sex
No sudden movements. Your calf will spasm;
followed by your back. When the spasm starts
put him at ease, laugh about it, assure him
it's fine, happens all the time. Repeat this
until he's calm, for as long as it takes.

Adulting

When I ache
I'm awake

*

Clutching my knee
like a stress ball

*

I used to be able
to climb the garden fence

*

A café cup flies
as my hand jerks

*

Reading Heaney
in the hospital corridor

*

A doctor calls me in,
says 'what happened to
you?'

*

Too painful
to play Twister

*

The brown envelope
squatting on the doormat

*

Wrist shakes enough
you can forget reading

*

Spasm sends my knee into
my face, jolts me awake

Appointment in Clinic K

That's where I was supposed to be heading
but I kept straight on and took two lefts
back to the Children's Waiting Room.
I stood at the blue door. The nurse said 'Can I help you?'
The Noddy mural was still on the wall,
the red wooden post van hadn't moved.

Kin

I was teaching and then I saw him,
out the window in his walking frame,
playing football with the other kids.
I saw the way his legs bent inwards, how his toes
touched the floor before the heel.
I wanted to catch his eye, have a chat,
show him my splints.

Keeping Up

Plodding in the shadow of a crag, you –
one of the last Cumbrians to get polio – say
'Mind your cane, the ground is loose here.'
Back in the car I realise you never overtook me,
always moved at my pace.

Arthur Honeyman's Birthday, 3am 1970

Arthur Honeyman wanted a pancake.
He was pushed by a friend who was deafened
by Vietnam. The waitress looks at them
and nods to her boss. She walks over.
'We'll get the pancakes,' Arthur's friend says.
The waitress stares, then looks at her shoes.
'You're disturbing the other patrons,' she says.
A family looks over. 'We only want the—'
but before Arthur's friend can finish the waitress says
'I can't believe that something like you
would come someplace where people are trying to eat.
I thought people like you were supposed to die at birth.'
Arthur turns to his friend and says
'Why is the waitress talking about you this way?
I don't think you look any worse than you usually do.'
Then the waitress says 'if you don't leave I'll have to call the police.'
'Go ahead,' Arthur said. 'Call them.'

Arthur Honeyman and his friend, Richard Pimentel, were arrested and found guilty of breaking an 'ugly law'. Ugly Laws prohibited 'any person who is diseased, maimed, mutilated, or in any way deformed, so as to be an unsightly or disgusting object' from appearing in public. These laws remained in effect in the United States from the 1860s to the late 1970s. A similar law was used as recently as 2004 in the UK, when a beggar who displayed a wound on his neck was issued an 'Anti-Social Behaviour Order' by Camden police, which banned him from re-entering the town.

Hospital Coffee

I order and the Welsh waitress says
'Do you want me to carry it over darling?'
'Yes, my hands can't be trusted.'
A white-haired man in a Hawaiian shirt
with a bristly moustache orders green tea.
A girl who can't be much older than twelve
is waiting by the empty wheelchair marked
'this belongs to O.C.D.U.' All the tables are low.
A man with a half-paralysed face has a Coke.
A boy uses an eye-tracking keyboard to speak.
I drink my black coffee slowly. No one stares.
My neck spasms, my head twitches
and I feel fine.

O.C.D.U. stands for Occupational Clinical Decisions Unit.

The Night Before My PiP Tribunal I See My Dead

You left a note.
'Please don't judge me
too harshly.' I read it
at your memorial.
I hate that my voice
didn't shake.
Your mum worried
she'd broken your knees
when she cut you down.
At the inquest
the embalmer said
it was obvious
you died in agony.
When your sister heard that
she went straight to the bar.
Three years' sobriety gone.
At your funeral it was just me,
your gran, the hired pallbearers
and the priest, who kept
thumbing his gown.
Bailiffs found your body.
Your cat was screaming,
they said. You were so thin.
They slid bags of sand
into your casket
so we could feel the weight
on our shoulders.
You would have
liked the crowd,
the thick procession

of callipers, canes, crutches.
The relatives always asked me
to speak. I was the writer,
I'd know what to say.
So many of my dead. After
twenty-seven funerals, I stopped
counting. At the last one
I held myself up
at the pulpit,
got through the usual words.
Faces like tea-bags
left out to dry looked back
at me. Sitting outside the church
we talked about your favourite
party trick, opening beer bottles
with your wheel spokes.

Dear Legs

who stared back at me
from the bottom of toilet stalls
when I'd slice a sharpened
protractor across your flesh.
You, sworn at under breath
on every steep staircase.
How many surgeons have held you
in their hands, got to know you
through X-rays and test results?
Background fridge buzz of my life,
I swim for the first time in years,
float and don't hear you –
O spastic diplegic legs, O lovely
twiglet legs that survived.

Notes

'Kin' owes a debt to Ona Gritz' wonderful poem, 'We Are Everywhere', which appears in her debut full collection, *Geode* (Main Street Rag: 2014).

'The Spastic's Guide to Sex' couldn't have existed without Jillian Weise's poem, 'The Amputee's Guide to Sex'. Thank you to Weise, and to the hundreds of disabled poets who have made my work possible.

'The Night Before My PiP Tribunal I See My Dead' is for all my friends who died benefit-related deaths. It is estimated that over 120,000 people have died as a result of austerity. At least sixty-nine suicides have been linked to the Department of Work and Pensions. In 2016, the UN reported that the Tories had created a 'human catastrophe' which has led to 'grave and systematic' violations of disabled people's human rights. At the time of writing, there is a call for a public enquiry into benefit-related deaths. If you want to know more about how it feels to exist as a disabled person in Tory Britain, I would recommend the following three books. They're heart-breaking but necessary reads:

Stef Benstead, *Second Class Citizens: The Treatment of Disabled People in Austerity Britain* (Centre for Welfare Reform: 2019)

Frances Ryan, *Crippled: Austerity and the Demonization of Disabled People* (Verso Books: 2019)

Ellen Clifford, *The War on Disabled People: Capitalism, Welfare, and the Making of a Human Catastrophe* (Zed Books: 2020)

Acknowledgements

My thanks to the editors of the following magazines and anthologies where some of these poems first appeared, often in earlier versions: *The Dark Horse, The North, Sick Magazine, Zoomglossia,* and *We've Done Nothing Wrong, We've Nothing to Hide: The Verve Anthology of Diversity Poems.*

An earlier version of 'How to Wheel' won third prize in Verve's 2020 Poetry Competition, on the theme of diversity. Thank you to Andrew McMillan for judging the competition and editing the subsequent anthology. Thanks to Stuart Bartholomew for running Verve with such cool, unrattled aplomb. 'I Have a Literal Mind' was a poster in the loos of the Cut Arts Centre. Thanks to the Poetry People for producing the poster, and to the Cut for putting poetry on the walls.

My deepest thanks to Gerry Cambridge, who saw many of these poems in their more unruly versions, and provided immensely helpful edits and commentary.

In the early days of the pandemic, Liz Berry offered to send writing prompts to people who were shielding. Her prompt booted me into writing 'Dear Legs'. The poem simply wouldn't have existed without Berry's gentle nudge in the right direction, and without that prompt, this book wouldn't have an ending.

If it wasn't for a writing workshop that I attended in Year 10, I would never have picked up a pen at all. Thank you to Dean for leading that workshop, and to the Leiston High English Department for bringing a bunch of rural kids to poetry.

Thank you to Dean and Naomi, who commented on these poems at every stage of their development. You both suffered through many, many truly awful poems from me to get to this point. You both saw the potential in strangulated drafts. For as long as I've been a poet, you've both supported my work. I'm always grateful that you two saw something worth persevering with in my poems. Thanks isn't a big enough word.

Many generous hearts were instrumental in making me the person who could write these poems. To Ms. Humphrey, the best SENCO anyone could ask for. 'First Meeting' is as much your poem as it is mine. To Mr. Kennedy, for making detention the first place where I could think. To Miss Kenny, Ms. Smith, and the entire Leiston High English Department, for encouraging me, always. You all said I would have a book one day, and it seems you were right! This one's for you.

Cheers to Dave, even though we never talked about poetry, our many coffees laid the groundwork for these poems.

A great deal of these poems began in the Cut Loose writing workshop, run by Michael Laskey and Dean Parkin. Thank you to Michael and Dean for creating such a rich, generative space for writing, and cheers to the Cut, for being such a vibrant local hub of poets and artists.

All the poems collected here have benefited from the keen, careful and thorough criticism of the East Suffolk Writing Workshop Group. These poems would have been baggier, shoddier pieces of work without your help. Thank you all for helping me be the best poet I can be.

Thank you to the many people who read this manuscript and offered extensive commentary: Michael, Dean, Naomi, Lucy, Steve, Polly, Hannah, Rob, Flo, Elspeth, Martin and Clive. Regardless of whether I took your suggestions on board or not, all your comments helped me know the poems better. Thank you all for your deep engagement with these small poems.

I'm grateful to everyone at The Poetry Business for bringing this pamphlet into being. I owe a debt of thanks to David Wheatley, Andrew McMillan, Joanne Limburg, Amy Mackelden, Raymond Antrobus and Ilya Kaminsky for taking the time out to say lovely things about this titchy book. Thank you to Kim Moore for seeing something in my little poems, and for judging the New Poets Prize amidst a global pandemic.

Thank you all, dear generous hearts. None of this would have been possible without you.

Finally, thank you, dear reader. A poem is only complete when it finds a reader. Thank you for completing these poems.

Thank you so much for reading this pamphlet. If this is your first encounter with disabled poetry, you might want to read more. Disabled poetry has never been more vibrant, searching, global and alive. Because I could happily quadruple the length of this pamphlet just by recommending books, here are just a few recommendations of where to start reading disabled poetry. If you want to learn more, or if you're looking for something specific, get in touch with me on Twitter: @inadarkwood

Tilling the Hard Soil: Poetry, Prose and Art by South African Writers with Disabilities, ed. Kobus Moolman (University of KwaZulu-Natal Press: 2010)

Beauty is a Verb: The New Poetry of Disability, eds. Jennifer Bartlett, Sheila Black & Michael Northen (Cinco Puntos Press: 2011)

QDA: A Queer Disability Anthology, ed. Raymond Luczak (Squares & Rebels: 2015)

Stairs and Whispers: D/deaf and Disabled Poets Write Back, eds. Sandra Alland, Khairani Barokka & Daniel Sluman (Nine Arches Press: 2017)

Imaginary Safe House, eds. Shane Neilson, Roxanna Bennett & Ally Fleming (Frog Hollow Press: 2019)